Ebullience and Other Poems

Ebullience and Other Poems

Poems by

Bhupender K Bhardwaj

© 2019 Bhupender K Bhardwaj. All rights reserved. This material may not be reproduced in any form, published, reprinted, recorded, performed, broadcast, without the express written consent of Bhupender K Bhardwaj.
All such actions are strictly prohibited by law.

Cover design by Shay Culligan

ISBN: 978-1-949229-80-6

Kelsay Books Inc.
kelsaybooks.com
502 S 1040 E, A119
American Fork, Utah 84003

For Chris Cornell;
Pooja, my wife, and V K Bhardwaj, my mother

Acknowledgments

First and foremost, I would like to extend my thanks to Karen Kelsay, MD of Kelsay Books for finding my poetry collection worthy of publication.

Also, I thank the editors of all the poetry magazines (listed below) in which my individual poems appeared:

Random Poetry Tree: "Haven"

Kingston Creative Writer's Blog and The Legendary: "Ebullience," "The Zone," "Winter Afternoons"

The Galway Review: "To Bring Back Memories of the Dead," "Through the Dense Passages of Loss," "The Sparkle of the Burnished Metal"

Mad Swirl: "When the Sloping Earth," "Bridging the Gap"

Poetry Life and Times: "The Sudden Drizzle"

Madras Courier: "The Meadows Poem"

Squawk Back: "Permanent Brightness"

Contents

Haven	11
Ebullience	12
Pastoral Snapshots	13
When the Fulgent Goats…	14
When the Sloping Earth…	15
The Sudden Drizzle	16
Winter Afternoons	17
The Zone	18
Opulence	19
The Bene Israel	20
Pristine Voyages	21
To Bring Back Memories of the Dead	23
Through the Dense Passages of Loss	24
The Sparkle of the Burnished Metal	25
The Meadows Poem	26
Enigmatic Night	27
Bridging the Gap	28
Clarity	29
Nature Lovers	30
Natural Empire	31
The Theatre	32
Magnificent Coliseum	33
Inheritance	34
Humility	35
Refreshed and Renewed	36
Permanent Brightness	37
Ars Poetica	38

Haven

There were ferns and beyond them
fields studded with bulky buffaloes;
their animated faces balanced
by their static symmetrical horns.

And on them, as if for visual effect
landed elegant egrets to have
their fill of ticks. Nearby, streetlamps
without lamps stood transfixed
giving a guard of honor
to the free-floating wind—noon's guest,
passing by with her retinue
of bees, dragonflies and flower-scents.

Propped up against the page of the sky
were the brown letters of the bricks
that forming into a kiln were fired
by the overhead furnace of the sun
so that its chimney tower, now defunct
frowned in disgrace. Truck ruts leading
to it were made home by muddy water
and buzzing flies idling over stagnancy.

This idyllic setting in a nondescript village
with its acres of cornfields and an abundance
of pastel blue clouds situated faraway
from the elite art of the barricaded galleries
is the common man's haven.

Ebullience

This path which has remained
undisturbed by the course
of civilization; with its boulders—
ancient prehistoric eggs beaming at you—

Zigzags down to the center
of your heart straightaway.
Dropping its altitude steadily,
it works its way with conviction

Through the dense grass, the wild
bushes, the lemon trees and lands you
in the folded palm of the earth
which is this vaporous valley

That sings with the sacrifice
of its soldiers who keep perishing
of harshness and its farmers
who gaily break their backs in the fields.

Here, where wheat stalks sway
in the sun of noon and the bees thrum
lazily, if you look closely
at the wooden plow
ranged against the furrowed field,

Between the initials deeply imprinted
on its worn-out handle,
your grandfather's spirit oscillating
with ebullience can be clearly discerned.

Pastoral Snapshots

That gnarled branch, the misshapen dragon that leaps
at you from the diminutive tree belches fire from its jaws
and it is sunlight. Lower down, the spider, goalkeeper of its nets
grabs the incoming shot of the insect and its movement
becomes sluggish.

Bring on the vision, the memory thick with brimming energy!
The paneled sky, an artwork which covered the inconsequential
villages extended the gift of perspective to its people that lives
however they were expended, amounted to powerful chronologies
of at least the minuscule self.

The undulating surface of water that ripples to the smash
imparted to it by the wind's sledgehammer has no history
but an everlasting present. Its concentric circles that radiate
outward in all directions alter the fate of electricity.
But this was an unleveled patch of grass-pierced earth
on which perched was the basil-crowned lighthouse—
guide to the seafaring people and meaning-seeking writers,
anchor of the universe; its side-enclosures lit each evening
with glowing lamps by that slender lady, resilient hunchback.
Her voice incorporated the cumulative history of our ancestors
and between the two lights of their cigarettes
and the cooking hearth placid boys and girls were raised
despite the brickbats hurled by fate at them.

In the distance, cattle munching on their fodder in the rusted barn,
creak of the pulley, water being withdrawn from the well
and the moonlight painting the thatched houses white.

When the Fulgent Goats…

When the fulgent goats scrape their sides against the brick wall
and trudge lazily along it, know that it is the weekend.
The hour sees the dragonflies skimming across the grass
and the season ball smashed by the batsman into the pavilion.

From the corners heaps of garbage are being cleared; double-edged
sword that slices advancement from incivility. While moustachioed
merchants pluck gold from the corn on the cob that in turn knocks
down the aurum from their avaricious teeth.

Plaits of thin fumes that decamp from the busy frying pans
worked by chefs remind you of your lady's stylish mane. A mirage
conjured by heat and smoke ferries you back to your origins
and astonishment takes root in your breath.

Those moments: the glorious passage of a pigeon scissoring
the blue and the skyline of the city visible from behind
a bay window are priceless.

Though the footsteps that paved the path between the picturesque
buildings of that age will become daubed with splashes of mud,
they will endure forever recorded in the land's memory.

When the Sloping Earth…

When the sloping earth within the latticed wooden perimeter
of the duck pond cracks open in spaces from the fierce heat
of the tropics it not only yields the anatomy of the wilted blade
of the grass but also the snapshot of its glowing core
that rotates nonstop. The wrinkled nightgown of water flows
down your woman's curved body of monolithic stairs landing
into the pond. The paper-white ducks freighted
with the foreknowledge of future wade thoughtfully;
the impending drought showing itself in their buttoned-up eyes.
Through the stiffened leaves lying scattered the wind steals
like a thief and raising dust that settles on eyelashes,
dictates the essay of stoniness.

Yearning with its cargo of incredible visions and perfumed
essences enters the world through two pillared gates
and bells tinkle sonorously in the ears of timorous hope.

The Sudden Drizzle

The sudden drizzle that brought long-sought fulfillment
to the scorched shacks of the country masses
knitted the serrated peak and the neglected pavement
into an aquamarine fabric under whose grace wild asses
brayed with glee. The rusted generator attached
to the cola factory hummed loudly and recalled
memories of the dull headaches which once latched
onto you. But these were phantoms of imagination which caught
you unawares in the coerced stillness induced by your drab work
that ate you up slowly, constricting your vision
beyond which strong-legged peacocks continued to jerk
their bald heads in unison with the swaying trees that season.

Later, the sparrow-squeaks and the marketplace shouts—
    matchless
which came up the moist verges, were glinting arrows that made
    you guiltless.

Winter Afternoons

Winter afternoons are terrific for their trademark light
which honeys down into every inch of space between you
and the objects, for the fluttering of worn-out flags rippling
from the masts erected on the ramparts of the colonial sports club.
They drum up the coppery leaves in the living room
of the splayed forest into a broadening music
which hypnotizes you within the parenthesis of your bony skull.
At this hour, when the shadows don't want to depart
from their owners, the balding hills with their hutments
appear afloat in mid-air lost in the maze of siesta. The smells
of roasted capsicum which bring greetings to weariness
and the vision of tragic goats ambling along the undulating
ridges sum up the essence of kindness.

The sunrays singeing your skin with patience instill faith in you
despite the innumerable cul-de-sacs your fate pushed you into.

The Zone

To be away from the fenced-in ventilated mental space
you call yours, to be distanced from the shuttered shops,
the cobblestones of the street and the blue meditating
between the gabled houses is to be in painful exile.

Removed become the routines that like a cave used to shelter
you from the cruel jabs disappointments gave. Earlier, the cold
milk swirling in your favorite glass used to mimic cosmos
and your German shepherd lapping up water from its customary
bowl pleased you no end. The evening strolls along the shaded
avenues always took you one step closer to enlightenment.
The world was one gigantic jigsaw puzzle; open to interpretation
whose pieces would fit in any way, after the slightest effort.

To relocate elsewhere, even if for a day made the hammer
of absurdity come crashing down on your head and the Boy
within would withdraw—a snail into its coiled shell.

Opulence

There is a carnivalesque pandemonium in the streets
because it is a Sunday. The day walks at such a slow pace
that desire stills itself into an archer's pose and releases
furious arrows of grass from the side-garden enclosures.
Silence nurtures you in its camphor-perforated teakwood bed
and in the bathtub, the tired body births itself
when it basks in warm water without let.
On the unforgettable pavements, lanky boys are spinning
colorful tops, while others zoom past on their bicycles
to dissolve into the electric air. The seller of ice-candies
is immortal for he mixes thunder and sunshine
in the colas he sells. And below the cantilevered bridge
which marries the two banks, the river flows like a girl's scarf
in the silky heat.

All contradictions get resolved in a split second.
The future glimmers with wide-eyed opulence.

The Bene Israel*

The scattered beach circled by the screeching gulls
is empty now and will begin to fill shortly as the evening
comes with its drama of silhouettes against the stamped-
yellow sky; where cigarette-ends will light the path
only to be outdone by the torchlight emitted by the fireflies.
And girls and boys with their hats on will gyrate to the drumbeats,
their felt hats whose inward silky circumferences will catch the fire
leaping from the logs of wood but these vacation-a-day tourists
catch no history of this coastal town of Alibaug as behind them
having navigated the course of centuries work about
the Bene Israel. 'O! I did not admit you fellow Israelis!'
the beach exclaimed. 'But I embraced you as my own kin.'

Their riveting synagogue that soars skyward, I want
my poetry to parallel the width of the heaven it touches.

'Our ancestors were oil pressers but of our heritage
what shall we utter?'
I too, shall press oil from the rig of existence
and write on these pages smelling
of petrol, of turpentine, of paraffin wax lighted
by one flambeaux lamp under the rusted iron shed
where once you moved in your autonomy;
write about their sea journey when two millennia ago
how they landed on our shores
without any collective memory
or heritage but with their Selves,
greater than any art or history or myth.

---

*Bene Israel: Historical sources state the Bene Israel are descendants of an Israeli ancestry which settled along the western coast of India about one to two millennia ago after being exiled from their capital Samaria by the Assyrian king Shalmaneser.

Pristine Voyages

1

He saw a hurried sort of compression visible about the way
the villas of the viceroys, the museums tired by the careless
treading of the transient tourists and the wooden bungalows
that echoed with the voices of generations groaning at the edge
of extinction—were arranged. Shimla, the empire's summer capital
was no longer the center from which hermetically sealed
envelopes with their carved royal insignia conveyed sternly-
worded messages
that dictated evil designs to be inflicted upon the masses. He saw
ruins of the decayed raj in place of the snobbish structures
they had raised all around. The sun rocking from side to side
like the clock's pendulum intoxicates him no end.
From the sturdy army schools, break time chats punctuated
by rollicking laughter resurrect his boyhood before him.

The conifers perched on the mountain slopes lob green grenades
at him and he feels it is a benediction just to breathe and be alive.

2

Now that he was finally in Lucknow, the city of nawabs
and the initial surge of disappointment had subsided
in the opaque thermometer of his body he decided it was time
to explore the marvels of that place. He walked persistently
at all the hours of the day; in the clarity of the noon
when the sun's javelins burned away his confusion,
in the evenings when the breeze rang the temple bell
with its sleek fingers. This sharpened his vision so much
that he became convinced that all that is of value in the world
is not what glittered in the storefronts but the peculiar bent
of the sunray on the wide trunk of the banyan tree.

To him architectural beauty was a bunch of roses
that painted the eye in red and the rows and rows of wheat stalks
but not the colonial legislature building
which was just an exclamatory mark of the past.

The adaptable tramp he was, Lucknow gradually became part
of his breath and bone and through the charms of the city
he reached his own cozy lair—his town surrounded by palm trees
lost behind tons of smoke.

3

The accumulating years of his uneventful life
through which he ran like a bull towards a red flag; except that
there was no flag in this case but the fiery disc of the sun
above a steady horizon was what he prized above anything else.
His skeleton became resilient to the blows rained
on him by the fickle element of randomness which drew him
into quagmires of deceit. What was vulnerable in him,
he sheltered it in a tough tortoise-like shell fashioned out
of sheer will and whose circumference he guarded from intrusions
with the persistence of a priest protecting the sanctum sanctorum
of an ancient temple. To him, the twirling leaves which the wind
energized meant more than any plush property and sleep
was a probing rod by which daytime's magic could be penetrated
from the night's laboratory.

In the brightness, he was an ambitious flaneur who loved
to skim the many avenues and by-lanes of the textbook
of his hometown, whose contents remained inexplicable
no matter how many times he glimpsed through it
but whose spirit his spirit completely grasped.

To Bring Back Memories of the Dead

To bring back memories of the dead
is the same as feeling tremendous guilt inside
on having reprimanded someone
for a thing they did not do.

Within the corridors of your mind
recreating the deceased,
you fill the gap their death left
with all their actions—right and wrong.

The ancient Jewish cemetery that stands
in front of me is home to my brothers
whom I never met.

The dead there evoke delicate feelings in me,
these feelings I realize
have revealed their grandiosity
in the snow-white flowers
that have bloomed on the overarching tree.

The invisible maroon-colored vintage wine
flowing from their dead bones,
which paints the world in various shades
has created the partition and is the no-man's-void
between life and death.

Through the Dense Passages of Loss

Through the dense passages of loss,
we kept moving and moving
believing a sunflower and honey bees hovering above it
would greet us at the end of our travelling.

The days were suffused with illusive hopes, all blending
into painful years that bore the indelible stamp of repetition
when in fact, our time on earth should have resembled a colorful
canvas painted with the essence of meanings.

We wrongly believed that our peace lay in what others
were doing—acquiring symbols of materialism, engaging
in queer talks, putting up a deliberate show of falsity.

Though we were situated in a hazy matrix of manufactured
cosmos; the joyous yelp of a dog, the immortal taste
of the sweet earth-colored tea and above all the hands
of the lover in our hands helped us endure the toughest ordeal
of surviving each passing minute.

The Sparkle of the Burnished Metal

The sparkle of the burnished metal, the stare of the greasy glass
bulb, the grim look of the matchbox should not be avoided
for they extend to us the wisdom of the ages through their silent
language which must be deciphered by us.

The gurgling silver dancing down the fountain is a silence full
of sounds: ungraspable, a nullity as when daydreaming you feel
the contours of a maroon-colored paper punch which you loved
in your childhood but the sudden ascent of a black ant
up your foot signals to you your person. There remains thus,
neither your childhood nor the paper-punch.

Which woman can face the horizon standing at level with it
and that too eye to eye? The woman who lives each Day
which erupts like a red fire from the rusted stove of the night
as if it was all: no vitality and decay preceding it and following it.

When you enter the heart of the spark flying from the knife
touched across the rim of the wheel, when you hear the pulse
of time like your own heartbeat you will see
yourself face to face i.e. nobody.

The Meadows Poem

Peer out through the latticed window
and you can see the spires of the gothic structures
erect as snooker cues.

The thumping music from the race cars
mesmerizes the spoilt brats with pierced ears
who sport sunglasses at night and chew tobacco casually.

There is jubilation in the air
and your eye is on the prowl
to capture a lost comrade's twitching face.

The lights are modern, projectors
around which the fog swirls
and the cinema of the road breaks its monotony
at the foot of the drug peddler who steals his Marlboros
from the locked modular cigarette shop.

The infectious energy of the night
has made the long-haired metrosexuals madmen
and they are pumping bullets in vacancy,
intoxicated by nothingness.

They think that it is their time,
that it will last forever.
Only the mongrels, keen observers
of human follies shake their muzzles
in knowingness.

Enigmatic Night

In the gloomy night
only the insects are heard
sounding their instruments.
At eye level, in dim light
one can spot ghosts floating;
their dimensions swiftly swallowed
by the hungry darkness.

The solitary street looks surreal framed
by the jacaranda trees. It's just like peering
into a dream through sleepy eyes from behind
a hazy curtain. As a drop of water
that escapes from the astronaut's mouth
to become a bubble, the moon has risen
too high escaping from the sea's body.

Etched permanently in the black sky;
it has locked lovers in a reverie,
the plants in a spreading shyness,
and has stopped the terrorists dead in their tracks.
The only sound is the thud
of their guns dropped forever.

Bridging the Gap

The self-possessed person who takes pride
in twirling his mustache, adjusting his necktie
and patting his wallet like a pet
is the poorest and the richest person
is the one who derives utmost pleasure
not from collecting the silver coins of the rain
that shower down incessantly from the mint
of the sky but from watching its darts
hit the earth's board and his heart
which is its bull's eye.

Why is it that one does not see
that the grave-edge of reason bruises
the face of happiness, that pretentious behavior
leads to ruination and a stomach ache
dissolves one's ego, pride and possessions?

After it has finished raining, pools of pristine water
that contain the sky, newly born trees and the turtle
floating downslope across rills say to us, "Only in
proximity to us, can you gain your lost self."

Clarity

The summer is finally upon us, time to flex and stretch our limbs like the crab. I am not there but I can see the flock of green-throated pigeons hovering above to scan the receding patches of water below to satiate their fierce thirst. The semi-ripe mangoes yield themselves to the tongues of their eaters who long to settle in the forest which though dense has room inside its branches to house everybody. The gutters on the side abound with filth and futility, water no longer sings in them. Only shards of glass and dehydrated grass jut out from them. While our motives and designs are scanned to the bone by the stripped light of the tropical sun.

The breeze that billows out from the horizon clears out the clutter from indolent minds and clarity hunts the charms and smells of this profound season.

Nature Lovers

Their squalid houses strung out along the hillside
raise a ruckus each morning by ramming into each other
like bulls but their poor inhabitants are concerned
about getting done the age-old daily chores of defecating out
in the bush, bathing under the blessed water of the standpipe
and brushing their teeth with neem-leaf. Their patient ladies
oil each other's radiant hair that lights up the dark alleys
of the slum settlement, scanned nevertheless by the green
headlamps of the nagging cat who surveys the locality
not for scraps of compassion but for slices of fish
which are her birthright.

Their jute-netted cots, their cobwebbed windows, their broken
stools on which cards were played spoke to me of a fairy tale
in which the golden silence got punctured only by the honking
of their twisted rickshaws and the petty fights of the newly-drunk
youths excited by their own cusswords. I smelled their damp
streets, the smells of their trousers and petticoats washed
with modern detergents which flapped like flags from the wiry
clotheslines and their typical bakeries that sold peppermint
and bread rolls. But I was getting nowhere nearer to them,
the eternal men of the land who lived in close communion with it,
whom no secrets of the night eluded and who in the daytime
were wedded to the shadows of the sunflowers and the palm trees.

Natural Empire

The clarion call of the ragged herdsman.
The march past of the energetic bleating goats.
The flags of the palm trees rippling in the noon wind.
The sunlight stamped on the rugged topography of the region.

The benediction of the flowing water stepping down the hillock.
The marble statues of the cows leaning into the grasses.
The skulls of hollow coconuts rolling into the soft abyss.
The long low clouds on their way through the highway of the sky.

From the clangor of the cement mixers and the industrial plants
I awoke to these marvels of the natural empire whose dominions
were not found plotted in the dog-eared pages of the school atlas
but spread out among the brown pages of the earth.

When these salubrious joy-sprinkling entities are shunned,
the croaking of the frogs cancels the clinking of the crockery,
the fierce bellowing of the bulls drowns the bikers' honks,
and the ancient wind that sculpts your face mocks the air-
conditioned men.

The Theatre

The ornate theatre built by the municipality with modern glass and striking exterior is a matter of pride for those who perform their plays aided by elaborate props and the strict sentries who control the entry of the public into the baroque era.

Yet the expensive attires and the eloquent speech that accentuate the obduracy of the actors only magnify their vanity. The façade of their false pride fortified by out of place embellishments crumbles before the all-pervasive theatre of the sky's dome punctuated by stars, which mesmerizes with the simplicity of the light's classical language and the gentleness of the wind's music.

This unparalleled theatre remains open forever and to gain admission no tickets are required—only a receptive eye and a fullness of spirit.

Magnificent Coliseum

Manacled by the rambunctious clematis,
tiptoed upon by the rust-speckled pigeons
these were the exemplary one-roomed tenements
whose roofs were the upturned coal iron-boxes'
blazing plates that ironed the blue fabric of the sky
with the determination of a one-man army
out to crumble a mountain into a handful of dust.
To a falcon plummeting down from a skyscraper altitude,
slashing the air with its powerful pair of wings
appeared this magnificent coliseum formed
from circular hills which like descending
terrace plantations came to be inhabited by men undone
by sluggish existence; rotten lives stained by betel nut
and pan masala but was not the new generation adamant
to set things right like an iron-box moving
across old clothes which warble like withered crops
suddenly supplied water after a summery hiatus?

There were signs, almost imperial of progress—
workshops manufacturing antique handicrafts,
statues of gods and cell phones together!
And how the erstwhile corners of gullies
that reeked of garbage now glimmered
with gold-lettered proverbs. This coliseum
that is touched by the tangent of the railway line
whose engine's soft gurgling sound is the same
as that emanating from the rust-speckled pigeon's
throat presently tiptoeing across the oven-hot roofs
of my tremendous town.

Inheritance

   for papa (1958-)

In the broad roadside dispensary
roofed with corrugated iron,
on the teakwood table
that shone with recent polish
were placed glass jars filled
with finely ground powders
and hexagonal stone pits loaded
with layers of herbs, honey
and cloves deposited alternately.

Clutching the chair, I, the timid child
was mesmerized by all this stuff of my father,
while he the doctor, almost squinted in concentration
engrossed in making formulations
that would liberate his patients from sharp pain.

Adept at drawing out the precise quantity
of the ingredients and mixing them up
in right proportions in little white-rimmed
bowls with grey bases, his hands created
their own music, though the pounding of medicines
resembled blackboards scraped by nails
or seawater splashed by oars.

Today, my father lives in me
and I feel him when I measure
out words to place in a poem
just as he did substances
in his mini-weigh scale
to prepare his medicines.

Humility

Beneath the shade of the rising surge
of deep-rooted gladness
that gives its thanks to incessant life,
construction workers congregated each day
in a makeshift eatery built of bamboo poles
and plastic boards covered by tarpaulin sheets
that somehow held together.

Amidst the cups of piping hot tea
enriched with black peppercorn
and green cardamom that were gulped
and gulped, freshness streamed across the faces
of those tired workers in the crumbling shop
even as they discussed rising costs,
sending meager finances back home
and the difficulties of putting up in an alien and a harsh city;
whereas buildings came up effortlessly about them.

When you stepped in, the warmth of their company
would infect you. A wada pav and a cup of tea
would be thrust into your hands, while your ears
caught their rustic Hindi like folk music.
For a while, you became a worker yourself
and all that big talk of changing the world
by big people would seem utter nonsense.

Refreshed and Renewed

The potted plant which you placed
in the corner of the grille
for me came to signify you.

So delicately its white-streaked pink rose
entered my heart and your name
was the fragrance I yearningly inhaled
and filled myself with daylong.

How immortally it stayed there
resting on sunlight's pillar,
how fervently it swayed
when the wind exalted it profusely.

The more I gaped at its multilayered petals,
the more magnetized I became
by the unplumbed aspects of your spirit-being.

When water sprinkled out from the pipe's nozzle,
I was refreshed and renewed.

Permanent Brightness

When the ribbed smell of fresh guavas
strikes you like a solid presence,
When the panther is in its element
and the parrots screech like rusted wheels,
When you are locked by the gaze of a bull
and come to be suddenly situated
in an eternal summer
(summer of table-top mountains that is circled
by the floating gondolas and schooners of memorable clouds),
then it is time for the spirit to leap from one glorious stone
to another like a spotted frog.
Can you dare to know what lies on the other side of the velveteen
curtains of the butterflies that slice the sun-lanced air?
Whether the chattering of the cicadas points to the possibilities
of what could be.
Whether we can ever replicate the creepers steady in their progress
toward an airy outpost.

The hum of the radio from the greased cycle shop
is matched by the buzz of the flies
and the jackfruit trees are happy
to throw their shadows on the languorous dogs.
Be perpetually indebted to the solid doorway of the limitless
that leads through the veranda to a permanent brightness.

Ars Poetica

Dotted along the bay formed by the racing strip of water,
toylike buildings huddle together not in a fraternal way
as trees but in a manorial style exhibiting a false sense
of grandeur imparted to them by their foppish architects.
These structures that loom overhead without cessation stare
into the mirror of the sea; their narcissism mocked by cottony
clouds, their counterparts in the azure sky that of their own
free will metamorphose into architectures of all the ages
from Gothic to Victorian to Saracenic. So the eye wanders less
into the labyrinthine streets formed by the elaborate sector-wise
set up of buildings that resemble stanzas of a poem where form
dominates content than the boundless sky which has room
only for the free verse composed by birds and clouds
whose measure is the trail of the horizon below
where content reigns over form.

May all works of art find their true balance like a glinting
coin that rotates on its shining axis and by combining freedom
and restraint in equal parts raise a monument
to this incomprehensible marvel called life.

About the Author

Bhupender K Bhardwaj was born in Mumbai, India in 1988. He is a poet and an essayist. A graduate in sociology from St.Xavier's College, Mumbai, he has been composing poetry since the last few years. He has worked as a bureaucrat with the Ministry of Railways, GOI for half a decade. His poems have been published by literary magazines across US, Europe and India. He was longlisted for The Toto Awards for English Creative Writing 2016 and shortlisted for the Poetry Society of India's All India Poetry Competition.

www.ingramcontent.com/pod-product-compliance
Lightning Source LLC
LaVergne TN
LVHW091322080426
835510LV00007B/603